MW01593116

THE BLIND GANDER

The Prelude to His Forthcoming

Contents

Chapter 1

Peace Makes Sense (Prelude Of The Blind Gander)

Peace All Over The World   9

Focusing On Him   11

Chancery Cursive   13

Short/Shorter   15

His Coming   17

Rivers Of Living Waters I   19

Rivers Of Living Waters Ii   21

Rivers Of Living Waters Iii   23

Rivers Of Living Waters Iv   25

Doubt   27

Rivers Of Living Water V   28

Summarize   29

Dancing In Life   30

Flying In-Love   32

Dancing With Love   34

Flying In Light   36

Holiness Is An Example-   38

The Promise Of Love-   40

Long/Longer   42

Tunnel Show   43

Chapter 2

A Praise Of Shift (Interlude Fo The Forthcoming)

Wide/Wider   46

Brief Labor Of Love   47

Deep/Deeper   48
Computer Consistency   49
High/Higher   50
High/Higher Ii   51
Deep/Deeper Ii   52
Deep/Deeper Iii   54
Deep/Deeper Iv   55
Deep/Deeper V   56
Sovereign God Of Love   57
Sovereign Margin   58
Shadows Of Now   60
Responsibility Clues   62
Maintaining Gravity   64
History Of-   65
Lampstands Of Tomorrow/The Future   66
Hens   68
Message Me   69
Higher/Lower   70

Chapter 3
Grace Moves (Conclude)

Info-Mercy   72
Plummets Of Grace   73
Resting Place Within The Waves   74
Wiring Tips   75
Blind Home   76
Brown Hope   77
Blind Prelude   78
The Prelude   79
The Brown Prelude   80

Preface

For some time now, I've been wondering what next to write or to give and to put out. Truthfully, I had no idea this would be the next book, until probably sometime in the middle of the year. I didn't know exactly what I'll receive, but while going to school, I felt compelled to write this.

The Holy Spirit was my chief inspiration, and chief director. He'd take me through class, and then after, through a writing session, and so on until this came out. I'm fortunate and thankful to have Him as my all.

The poems have a different tone as compared to the previous Blind Gander. Looking at them now, I realize they have a real childlike perspective to them. As such, I believe everyone can read it, from pre-teenagers to the oldest generation. Also, any race, religious affiliation, or denomination is catered to, within these poems.

Thank you for reading this, and God bless you as you enjoy the book.

Acknowledgement

I take this opportunity to thank my church, the Word of God Alive Ministries of Houston, Texas. It is expressively a joy to be part of you, and I'm thankful for all.

I thank Pastor Sidney and Pastor Dominic, who are like fathers to me, the ministers, and all the members of the church.

My friends (you know yourselves, 'Ivo and Florence', we are going to "Heavenly Places"), Chinaza and Ugonma. My family, my aunt, my uncles . Mom--we'll see each other soon, my brother too.

I especially thank Richard and Obi, who were part of this journey, though unbeknownst to them

Special thanks to Mrs. Oluwafisayo Fayiga of prowebxpression.com, for your extensive work on designing and putting this work together. God bless you Ma'am.

God Bless You All!

Dedication

I dedicate this poetry book to my Father in Heaven and my Lord and Savior Jesus Christ. You gave this me, and every other thing I possess, so thank You for this one, and for the many more I pray to give back to You.

This, and all I do, to You, Dearest LORD.

I love You, Holy Spirit!

CHAPTER 1

PEACE MAKES SENSE
(Prelude of The Blind Gander)

PEACE ALL OVER THE WORLD

All o'er the world,
beyond the circumferences.

There's an establishment,
a tradition,
a ritual,
embodying a burden.

Some sight/flight/right for a
blind bird with an understanding,
to uphold.

Between his contrasting wings,
he has found the right sound to
span out his forthcoming.

He realizes the comet he faces.
He is faster than his past,
when he drives ahead of his
shadow.

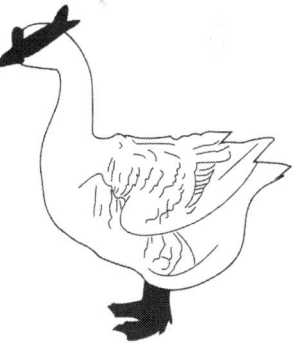

So with a summary that is little,
much less little,
littler, if that is a word,

The Blind Gander ..... The Prelude to His Forthcoming   9

than the qualification to pick up
this banner of white variations
and perceptions.

Clouds jubilating,
the addresses heading headlines headlong
for the addresses,

Peace all over the world
The heart of the whole meets the
opportunity after the parlay
of the bird, his eyesight,
his faith, pain, withdrawal
and subsequent resurrection.

FOCUSING ON HIM

Late night, late hours,
Late culture, late showers.

Mighty is His Power,
Perfect is His Wisdom

Late scouts, late routes,
Late reports, late/delays.

When the sighting is on the Way,
by the Lighting Off Him,
the corner is the stone for the next
throw.

While the efforts are seem-less,
the response is the Glory.

Who wouldn't want to focus all
on Him,
His Light, His Love, His Laughter
and His Joy?

I'm sorry, my story continues,
and did so even after the first

shuttle made the space headlines
from the imagination standpoint.

But real is now,
and 'tis so is time.
No one is waiting for me,
but God needs me to be
Focusing on Him,
or else every waiting list
gets longer.

God help me.
To focus on You.
To wait on You.
To wait on You.

CHANCERY CURSIVE

Even with me curving my
thoughts,
I can't curve wise ones.

I'll bend back into flight
elementary,
whereas these shades are
heading to brighter pastures-

Last night,
I fell head over heels
into Perfection, and found
out that my wings flap
sideways,
a little too much on the
left, and maybe more on the
right,
or in a leverage of in between.

The circumstance predicts
this development,
I have no right to bend
anything,
not even the letters of these

words.

Meeting the junction at hand,
I'm climbing the ladder of
steadfast hill to the
originality of words and
The Chancery Cursive of
Clever meditation.

God is in this House,
I must listen perfectly
to the letters of His Voice.

SHORT/SHORTER

If the Cross where standing on
one side,
and eternity on the other,
where would the
turquoise flame of favorite
understanding burn from,
and with what reasoning?

Where will the shelter be,
Or the canopy for the
main-rib/mainframe/
main-head for the
blind gander to perch
for divinely inspired
Focus?

Can I recite every wind's fan,
against my wing span,
for a ring's hand
or finger,
when the day draws
nearer?

I am short of understanding

The Cross or eternity,
but shorter at knowing
the time and distance of
it all.

Cloudy put, the choice of
the Wind is for my wings
to respond to the
Voice within.

Jesus is talking/silence.

HIS COMING

Go to the Blind Gander's
Coming/or his forthcoming.

But herald his entrance with
a torch of love and a
touch of hug and
a bunch of logs for his
feet to land on.

In the past, he was quieter,
Now he is silence.
In the present, he is silent,
He is preparing.
In the future, he is prepared,
Then he is coming.

In his absence, he writes
his memoirs in careful
leaves of which some,
he finds comfortably
to mend into a nest for
a home for his head.

Then his bread and his

water, he prays into.
He flies into the
delivery box, only to
read the same letter
every day beside his
lunch-
Time is coming.

You are going into-
your coming.

RIVERS OF LIVING WATERS I

Where do I drink when I
take a perch,
or where am I drinking
as I fly before and after
a light's speck?

What choice is more, where like a
dove or raven,
I find un-dried rivers,
un-drying rivers,
to make my home after the
stormy nights?

What is the occasion at hand,
for a drop to lead to the
springing up of a waterfall,
whereas I'm drunk
at the first sip of Life,
for life?

I'll ask enough questions to
fly just within the answering
range, but I must realize that
such waters have Light,

hence I'm flying beyond
the darkness of my
blindness,
into the brightness
where I must become a
Lightning witness?

What choice do I have,
except to drink and drink
and drink until the Rivers
give me the choice to bathe,
bathe and bathe,
until my eyes come alive,
for eternity,
and to see beyond the scale value
of my feet.

RIVERS OF LIVING WATERS II

I'll say I'm flying above greatness.
I'll say I'm beyond my fears.
I'll say I'm going beyond boldness.
I'll say I'm flying away my tears.

But I must say not flying
above these Rivers,
or flying beneath them either.

I'm learning to be submerged
in Life,
I'm becoming a submarine of
Living Virtue.

I drink at the well,
well, I prefer the rivers.
but for a quick stop,
the safest exit is beneath
the well,
where my reflection
ripples but in-stills my rest,
even though I can't see
beyond the strength of my
breast.

So, what choice do I have?
I guess if I stay long enough
within the Rivers,
sure enough,
my feathers and choices
will begin singing Truth,
even as my shadow is
learning suit.

RIVERS OF LIVING WATERS III

Rivers of living waters,
washing against my mind.
Again I say,
Rivers of Living Waters,
washing against my mind.

Washing against my wings
I have no fangs,
but washing through
my beak,
and flowing into my
brain as fluids for
thoughts.

At the last nick of time,
the elbow of the
incoming river meets
memory.

There is a juggle and
tussle and a
quandary is created
where Love
must come forth.

The Blind Gander ..... The Prelude to His Forthcoming

Sure enough, a
watery elbow is
sharper than a
Wavy Bed of dreams,
hence, I run the
course of falling
into Love again
and again,
for Love's sake.

What choice do I
have,
to be a flying
bird,
or a sinking
word?

RIVERS OF LIVING WATERS IV

As I close my eyes,
I see a dark, and
small river flowing
out and away.

Then, then,
a bigger, better-looking,
Lovely and light-giving
River rushes in.

The mirror it brings,
is the memory I need.
The song it sings,
is the vision I breathe.

The Answer it carries,
is the purpose I respect.

The One it reveals,
is the Love of Hope, I confess.

'I AM no respecter of persons,
But I love everyone to respect
Each other,' says the LORD.

The Blind Gander ..... The Prelude to His Forthcoming   25

I drink this in,
knowing fully well my cup
is just running over,
well, rivers,
I meant to say.
Rivers of Living Waters.

DOUBT

Doubt destroys,
it hates faith.

It loathes God's Word,
and sacrifices fate.

Where is God?
Right here in my heart.

Where is doubt?
Out there in the dark.

STAY, ALWAYS IN GOD'S LIGHT.

RIVERS OF LIVING WATER V

Beautiful, greenery,
Perfection, eternity.

Victory, majestic-al
Supreme, Rest simplicity

Digestion, exquisite
Cup, one of a Living Water diet

Silence, the gushing of the flows
Peace, the ecstasy in Love's Life.

Right, 'drinkable Life'
Light, 'drinkable ride'

White, 'Purity's port
Everlasting, Indigestible sight.

Purple, the King's River
Mellow, the King's Scepter

Humble, the King's Waters
Ready, the King's Living Letters

The Blind Gander ..... The Prelude to His Forthcoming   28

SUMMARIZE

A blind bird flying
over Light letters

-A wild bird flying
Over Life setters.

-Large books with
Extraordinary-size prints.

-Letters, phrases, on commas,
Full stops for ins.

-Witness, my witness,
I am a witness.

-Vision, Victory,
Love/Light writes this.

DANCING IN LIFE

Listen.

Dancing with Life,
hand-in-hand,
dancing in encouragement
wing-to-span.

Life is round,
clueless, if you are walking
backwards,
or dancing after-way-wards

But Life is found,
when Light is round,
where the blindness around
the circles of my eyes,
dance away,
at the Rising of the Sun.

When He comes each day, at
His appointed time,
my wings flap in gaiety.

When He arrives at the door of

my heart,
my fears do-distant in
mobility.

When He hugs my weak frame,
and I receive His strength,
I'm whole over again for
the moves into eternity.

-I am dancing with Life.

-Jesus, He is.

FLYING IN-LOVE

A while to love,
A ride in Love.

A while in Love,
A wife to love.

A beauty to cherish,
Beauty is cherishing.

-Beauty is fulfilling,
even as Love is everlasting.

Looking into His Eyes,
I must admit
I have been growing faint
because flight classes
Have been on limit.

-Laugh softly, LORD,
I am coming, long ahead
strong at head, if You let me
and as You do
day long for bread.

Don't let me, fly less,
LORD,
or over shallow waters,
where my brown eyes
see the empty bottoms
and think it's Light and Love.

Only in the Cloudless Realm of
Your Love,
do I find adequate and
sufficient flight, and enough
Rest and Sleep for the
Continuous ride.

As I shake my feathers at You in Love,
Hold them gently, LORD, and my beak
Too, as I realize that flight and love
and flying in love,
is waiting on You.

Love flies, wait…

DANCING WITH LOVE

Dancing with Love,
Dancing in Love.

Growing and dancing,
The change is above.

The change also,
The atmospheric greeting.

The compassion dance steps,
Plural for the
Everlasting musical notes.

Jumping up at times,
Learning to be still.

Walking off at times,
God loves me still.

Hold me close, my Lover,
And never let me go.

Teach me how to dance,
Your Love-steps.

Teach me to take this chance,
Your Love helps.
Teach me why You dance,
Your Love sets.
Teach me to receive every chance,
Your Love's best.

ALWAYS,
EACH AND EVERY
DANCE SESSION.

ALWAYS,
LOVE GIVES.

FLYING IN LIGHT

Therapeutic,
Treatment of order.

Visitation,
Wisdom of Another.

Vehicle of influence,
Traffic school of the air.

Excellent in wonder,
God of everywhere.

Flying in Light,
A view of wonder.

Legs behind me,
My blind fears must surrender.

Light is the wind,
I am the cloud.

LORD, You are my Wind,
Lightning my way off south.

Amen to You,
Amen to You Jesus.

My praises I augment,
My pen shouts,
Perfect peace inks out.

Amen,
LORD.

HOLINESS IS AN EXAMPLE-

Holiness is not a message,
Holiness is a lifestyle.

Holiness is not a passage,
Holiness is a life-ride.

Right now,
in the quarter mile of
an hour,
the moment enters a
never ticking-off stop.

The result is the goal of
a heart's quest,
-to meet the junction
of a higher beginning,
-a higher and steeper
climb up the ladder,
-a definite and sudden
change of life,
which began the last
past four years.

Hence, the message is

relevant when the
Promise is heard.
See, the Love is different.
I'm born blind, but I
see history through
dark eyes,
the present through
Lovely Love's Ways,
and tomorrow-
Ah tomorrow,
is too promised not
to be true.

I'm promised Love-

Jesus gave that to me,
the day my blind eyes saw His Cross.
My wings could only lead me that Way-

THE PROMISE OF LOVE-

The Wedding Day has been set.
The rainbow with the promise
of Lent,
with the preservation of
certain churches, denominations
of hearts, souls and saints.

Then, through the vehicle of the
Resurrection, I am
becoming a son of Light.

I am distant from past faults,
learning to fly steeper and
higher over past vaults,
as I heed the deepest memory
of them all-
Love set me free on a
Sunday morning,
two years ago.

Love did that to me,
set me free into the
high rock climbing
unto Mount Liberty,

so what's the un-prevalent
promise?

What am I so worried about,
or should be concerned
of.

This isn't a question.
but a statement,
so and hence why worry,
when
Love has already given me
more,
and promised me all,
HIMSELF?

LONG/LONGER

The shorter the tide,
The longer the effort-

The shorter the tie,
The longer the purpose.

The straighter the fire,
The hotter the burn,

The hotter the fire,
The longer the yearn.

Where am I flying to,
Being that I'm blind?

TUNNEL SHOW

Beneath the anguish
Beneath the tunnel
Beneath the fire,
There is a hope.

Beneath the darkness
Above the weakness
Beneath and above,
There is a rope.

On the other side of the humble,
Beneath peer pressure,
By the side of Love,
There is a show.

While all makes sense,
We don't see through,
Faith is bittersweet to laziness,
There is a Goal.

The tunnel show begins,
but the Glory of Life
is everywhere.

Eyes opening,
Where am I,
Flying to?

CHAPTER 2

A PRAISE OF SHIFT
(Interlude For The Forthcoming)

WIDE/WIDER

Broader than the
infrastructure to believe,
but wider than the
architecture of hope,
what is this,
what's furthermore,
farther all,
foremost?

Who's farther than the
method or report
to sing of Love,
or to be in Love,
as in being with Love,
forever and ever
in the wonderful
Wide/wider Presence
Of the Beautiful
God of the Heavens and
Earth and Universe?

I'll cancel the shortened
end.
But my mind is getting
wider?

BRIEF LABOR OF LOVE

I thank You Jesus
for loving me.

I'm too small for such
Extraordinary,
Extravagant,
Extra-magnificent
Love,
And gestures.

Where are You coming from,
My LORD,
Eden is waiting for me?

The Blind Gander ..... The Prelude to His Forthcoming

DEEP/DEEPER

Wider too,
The choice is greater.

The favor is deeper,
because the Color
is bluer.

The originality is different.
It is perfect.

He is Righteous,
the vision is perfect too,
for the version is righteous.

God moves in deeper ways,
hence the depths see
a different echo,
because each time
The Voice comes out,
the message is clear
and cleared for
eternity.

Deep, right.
Deeper, right?

COMPUTER CONSISTENCY

Colorful mishaps,
why because of
costly syntax.

Hence, combination recounts
equals the
computer rebounds.

By consistency measures,
thanks to the
merit-able pre-counts.

Hence, the digestible endeavor
is to surrender to
the Message of all time,
even as you type this-

HIGH/HIGHER

We are jumping over the
sounds of the glasses' voices,
we are going higher.

We are dreaming deeper with
the staircase of Jacob's journey,
we are growing higher.

We are higher than our
forefathers' past,
we are in a Higher Hope.

We are coming of age
to see high things,
our boat is going up a Higher Slope.

Thank you Jesus.

HIGH/HIGHER II

Heavenly regions,
Heavenly encounters.

Are there forests in Heaven,
LORD,
Heavenly adventurers?

How high can the mountains
reach,
if there is no sky?

What is the shortest entity,
below the sky of
earth,
for the money's worth
of time enjoying the
enrolling formula of
Eternity?

DEEP/DEEPER II

Is there a deeper sea
than the deep in Your
Heart, Father?

Is there a more deeper
reach in Your side,
Jesus,
than what You received
for my sake on Calvary?

I could journey to the end
of the vertical earth,
but horizontally, I couldn't
go any deeper,
for there is no such a thing.

How deep is Your Love for me,
How deep do You Love me?

My answers are short,
Your kisses deeper.

My heart is blunt,
Your hugs are deeper.

My mind is coming forth,
Your Light is pulling deeper,
My heart is learning love,
Your Love is…deep/deeper.

DEEP/DEEPER III

The Blind Gander's perspective-
Well,
Love is shortsighted,
even though I might be.

Well,
maybe I am,
I am counting my
foot-descents backwards.

I'll fly deeper,
of course.
I'll see deeper,
in course

I'll love deeper,
with course,
I'll be deeper
because,
Love is deeper,
in me.

Thank You Jesus,
I like, I see.

Amen.

DEEP/DEEPER IV

The clergy speaks-
well,
we must see deeper,
for our God is Truth.

We are fortunate,
our robes are bloodier
in cue.

We are dimensional,
we preach to keep others
off the pit-from-the-pull.

We are sinful,
make mistakes.

God's Blood washes over our
heads,
we must learn to walk deeper into
the wounds.

DEEP/DEEPER V

The Blue's Truth-
Love is blind,
is an understatement.

Love sees,
Look at me-
an understatement.

But Love pulls quietly and deeper,
look at me-
my dressing, Love's statement.

The Holy Spirit of Love is
The Love of God,
For Love is God,
Don't look at me-

Love is our deeper, eternal state-
ment.

SOVEREIGN GOD OF LOVE

I give You thanks Jesus,
For everything.

For loving me, trusting me,
Hugging me, touching me,
Leading me, teaching me.

God is sure in His Sovereignty,
He is Perfect in His.

I am sure, He is waiting for me,
push me LORD,
ever so gently,
to the promise side of
Love,
where it casts light shadows of
every
which way path I take,
because the burden of Love
is to take me into
Everlasting.

I love You LORD,
Thank You for all.

SOVEREIGN MARGIN

Gender oriented,
Gander superintendent.

Accustomed to hierarchy,
Component of surrendering
to Sovereignty.

In as much as the tenure of
the sky,
lasts with the margin of its wings,
its desperation for Glory
is unsurpassable.

It grazes for grace in
places of waste for
Messages of praise to
the God of Great.

Then, with another component
at wing,
learning of the Sovereign
Margin,
and surrendered to apostolic
coverage,

the conquest entails the
Journey through the skyline
fields of its present,
past its history
into the inevitability
of tomorrow's entity/
the eternity of forever more
and the Presence of
History's God.

SHADOWS OF NOW

By now,
instructions are
embedded in me.
With a view of
a blind slate
called ink and a
ready-made glass for
drinking called
imagination's lake,
clearly the fire of dawn
brings enough pages
of wisdom for a
perfect representation
of everything.

As in Heaven,
so it should be here in
earth,
hence now in Heaven,
now in earth.

Love in Heaven,
Love on earth.

Light in Heaven,
Light on earth.

History in the making,
Shadows of now.

Entities in the marking,
Going in the clouds.

Our pasts are behind us,
please, create a
better tomorrow out
of today's paste of
Benevolence.

RESPONSIBILITY CLUES

Just as a jurisdiction has
a margin,
so does responsibility lines
a marginal rhythm.

With subtle clues of
adjustment and conclusive
persuasions, responsibility
clues up and out,
and above and without,
all correspondences,
to wake up and break off.

Be the effort to shake the
bed of dawn,
and walk the clock out
for an hour run.

Be smart in responding to
Time as it reveals itself
by the chances given to it.

Even as a pair of wings
are spread-ed and digest the

cosmos and the wind's
echoes,
they know, they know,
they know the message.

FLY-KEEP FLAPPING
OR YOU FALL.

KEEP PERCHING
OR YOU FALL

KEEP FLYING
AND THE SKY
BECOMES SMALL.

MAINTAINING GRAVITY

Mesmerized by nothing,
even as the sky of imagination,
imagines a stigma/of a difference
of everything,
born under Heaven.

Nothing is small even when
magnified,
hence nothing is in need
of being magnified
if maintaining gravity is
its prodigy.
In respect to modesty
and thanks' titles and
melodies of music,
blues and waiting lists,
the prelude entails
how long it'll stay up,
and how high its
blindness/humility will last.

HISTORY OF-

Sometimes the greatest journey
began at a full stop.
The next one began at a
comma, a toss and the
whim of an exclamation mark.

To point at an outsider
for reason is insane,
thus the mediocrity of any
believer is not from God,
but by the size of the
pipeline of their dreams and
the points at which they
point for direction.

We are not grammatical errors,
But God writes us
out clearly.

LAMPSTANDS OF TOMORROW/THE FUTURE

I'm looking ahead-
I see.
I can see.

Do not mind my blindness,
there aren't any cataracts,
just differences in the
renewability of my
mind's abstracts.

No calluses on my mind-frame,
my fingertips and palms
have a Light of Reason.

Amongst the renewed drawings
and peripheral insights,
it'll take hindsight to
foresee the lampstands
at the distance.

Even as the cataracts are changing
into different embankments
that see the browner-s and
prowess of hope and the

Wisdom of first services,
the camera must roll on,
actions must take place
for the Light meltdown to candle wax.
(Come down from Heaven)

There becomes one task of
these feathery blisters
of my wings-
fly to the subsequent
lampstand for the
next direction.

The distance is eternity,
the time is the aura
to blind.

HENS

They fought,
red minds and
white skins.

Henceforth,
red wines and
wine skins.

We'll drink when
we eat our
meals at
dinner times,
precisely
and not at
seconds late of
mediocrity.

MESSAGE ME

Call me,
but give me your
number first.

Make sure, you
hear in and
believe within.

Message me,
but give me your
ears.

Your heart will
wear service,
as your spirit will
bear witness.

Hear me,
but give me
Your eyes.

I'm flying in
soon, real soon/for now.

HIGHER/LOWER

By and by,
I am coming to the
end of my journey.
This one at least.

Where I must digress-
My law to see before
I believe must.

My faith is my support
system,
depending on how high
or low I get.

Thus, a higher degree
I'll fly,
a lower sentence of doubt
I'll write.
I fight for freedom.

CHAPTER 3

GRACE MOVES
(Conclude)

INFO-MERCY

I must admit,
I NEED Him.

I can't fly any
higher without it.

For your information,
I'm graduating
yesterday.

Thus, by info-mercy
I'm flying up the
aisle the way
this prelude
has prayers of
thanksgiving to say.

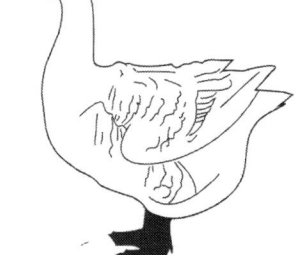

PLUMMETS OF GRACE

What makes this climb
sweeter is the taste
of grace.
Against my tail fronts,
I go higher by
the Power in the paste.
I'm learning to go
deeper into His
Loving Heart for
renewed taste.

My plummets have
and need more
behind,
as I go above and
beyond,
I'll leave trails of
His Grace.

RESTING PLACE WITHIN THE WAVES

There is a resting place
within the waves,
no one can find it
without learning to
praise.

While the sun shines in
each and every place,
there is a resting place
within the waves.

So in the different tongues
and foreign lips,
we'll find the place
of repose.

By the Spirit of God
The Father, the rest of the
Son's righteousness
gives us the ways
to be composed.

WIRING TIPS

Warring the legislature,
billing the law,
loving the respect,
respect in love.

These aren't taps but lips,
for your faith to print into the deep.
The lesson of wiring your trust
in dip,
the pressure of the bread to
be warmed without heat.

In exchange of the game,
of the table,
the choice is to see less
of nothing,
hear less of nothing,
and be nothing in the
tap of God's wiring.

The Blind Gander ..... The Prelude to His Forthcoming   75

BLIND HOME

Anchored on the purity of the
Word,
before the Light becomes my path.

Attached to the letter Word of Jesus,
for the blind mind to see the
fading manual of the 'graft.

Perfectly spoke, perfectly put
Hope given, hope cooked.
Heavy breathing, hope moved,
Light breathing, blind proof.

BROWN HOPE

Dust is such,
brown is common everywhere.
Hope is pure,
dust is seen anywhere.

Labor is strengthened,
Hope is grateful.
The brown hope of the last
century,
the commonwealth of the
last hopeful.

A beauty in the making,
dust is the marking everywhere.
In every mapping.

HOPE IS ALIVE.
STAYING ALIVE.

BLIND PRELUDE

Blind Prelude,
last motor.
Last motor,
blast method.

Brash sector,
For-Risen Savior.

Entity for an antennae,
an allowance for
centering.

Becoming in the beginning,
the beginning is the
becoming.

Always,
thus, the blind prelude
precedes the precedent.

The blind precedent awakes
the journey for the blind hunger
and subsequent everlasting
Supper.

THE PRELUDE

Before the journey begins,
there is a starting point.

Before the starting point,
there is a mark.

Before the mark,
a stop and readiness
enrolls.
Then the go becomes
satisfactory,
in as much as the
forthcoming is a
reshot sound away.

The Prelude awakens
the sprinter, runner,
listener or you,
the reader.

Love.

THE BROWN PRELUDE

Only in hope was this born,
to come alive in months,
fort ahead,
and forth to spread.

Away and always on
the pray-to-go,
sometimes and in some ways,
the message is to listen
to rest.

The starting point of above
is before this,
hence before the last point,
this poem has hope-
The brown prelude
for another,
and tomorrow's.

SHADOWS OF ENTITY

Footprints of destiny-
on the shoreline that
leads to eternity.
Welcoming in the exact
representation of Another,
becoming like Him,
means finding out what's
within.

Without any shadow of doubt,
Perfection lies within.
Without any shadow of doubt,
faith doesn't have a weekend.
Without any shadow of doubt,
God is Overall and Sovereign,
without any shadow of doubt,
a life without faith is weakened.

By Another's Act of
benevolence,
we are coming past
the essence.
It is original to be patient
for eternity,

being an umbra of God-
His companion,
in now's society.

There are no black plagues, but
the plate on my wall,
means I'm learning a different
language.

You too, for eternity.

Your arrival is inevitable,
for God is All Time,
you are Shadows of
Entity,
of His Excellency.

Conclusion Prayer

Thank You Father, for the summary of this life,
Thank You Father, for it has pleased You
to teach me how to fly.
I'm beginning where I left off Father,
to the sunrise of the dreams that never end.

Thank You Jesus.

Thank You for the Blind Gander,
He is growing up, all grown up,
He is moving up, all out,
He is moving out, all now,
He is flying away, too soon,
but never before his prelude.

Amen.

THE BLIND GANDER-The Prelude to His Forthcoming

Tomorrow has begun to stop the past history. The present has its circumstances, but flight by a blind perspective involves the collaboration of trust, love and the simplicity of a childlike faith. Life goes forward every day, and time comes forward too. We move forward too, and Truth moves us along His Way. We come toward the standpoint where we are lifted up beyond the previous and unto the elevated platform where our hope is nursed continually by the Light we do not see, but we see when our eyes are closed.

This is who we are, who I am, and who The Blind Gander is, and his prelude. He began ago, but continues on. He was a child then, but he is growing now. Much has changed, but all moves on. The effects of his movements characterize his prayers; all blind, all anchored towards his Faithful God, all empty without the breath of the Holy Spirit, and all irrelevant without the pleasing faith to fly blindly.

Originally from Cameroon, Teke Monono is a talented writer as well as a student in the University of Houston-Downtown. He has soared through many of life's challenges and come out a veritable winner. Furthermore, he has used these challenges to inspire him in his writing. Aside from this book, he is author to the previous Blind Gander. Currently, Mr. Monono is a student at the University of Houston. *Thank you LORD for this one!*

Made in the USA
Charleston, SC
04 August 2012